CONTENTS:

UP CLOSE

NOSES
That PLOW and POKE

Diane Swanson

GREYSTONE BOOKS

DOUGLAS & MCINTYRE PUBLISHING GROUP

VANCOUVER/TORONTO/NEW YORK

What a whiff! People can easily smell the sea on crabs and other critters that live there.

ALL KINDS OF NOSES

Who's nosy? Lots of animals are. They have noses for talking, noses for poking around— even noses for doing tricks. Of course, they also use a nose like you do: to breathe and smell.

As you breathe, you let fresh air in and stale air out. You also pick up smells along the way. But when you really want to smell something, you sniff deeply. You suck the air right up your nose to a mass of tiny smell sensors— about 16 million of them!

Nose hairs catch the dust you breathe in. When you sneeze, dust can jet back out at 160 kilometers (100 miles) an hour.

Although you can smell well, many animals can smell better. Bears have a super sense of smell that helps them find food. Black bears and grizzly bears can sniff out squirrels that are running underground. Polar bears can smell seals that are swimming beneath snow and ice.

The nose of a fish works full time as a sniffer, leaving all the business of breathing to its gills. Most fish have an especially keen sense of smell. A shark can sniff a few drops of blood from a distance equal to three city blocks. A salmon uses its nose to help find the way home. It swims hundreds of kilometers (hundreds of miles) upstream to return to the place where it hatched.

Some noses warn their owners of enemies. Bison can smell danger long before they see it. And the nose of a rabbit works as an early warning system: it has more than six times the number of smell sensors your nose has.

Wolves can smell prey that is 2 kilometers (more than a mile) away.

A mother bat can follow her nose to sniff out her pup among thousands of others in a nursery.

This polar bear is putting its super sniffer to work, checking the air for smells of food.

Yummy, a leaf salad! A long nose makes it possible for this African elephant to feed from the branches of trees.

TRiCky NoSeS

Tilt your head back and balance an eraser on your nose. With practice, you can balance a pencil, too. But even that wouldn't impress a sea lion. It can toss and catch driftwood with its nose—and swim at the same time.

Still, there's no nose trickier than an elephant's long trunk. Not only does it breathe in air, it sucks up water, then squirts it into the elephant's mouth. Sometimes an elephant uses trunkfuls of water to take showers. That's one way of keeping cool as well as keeping clean.

Part of the tip of the elephant's trunk moves like a nimble finger. It's great for picking up food, such as berries, grass, and leaves. It can also clutch a stick and scratch the elephant's itchy back. It can even soothe a

An elephant's trunk can hold 7 liters (1.5 gallons) of water. That's enough to fill two-thirds of a bathroom sink.

young elephant, called a calf. Calves suck the tips of their trunks just as human babies suck their thumbs.

Another big animal with a tricky nose lives in warm seas. The dugong (DOO-gong) feeds on underwater grasses and roots with the help of its nose. At the end of this nose, there's a movable disk that looks like a horseshoe covered with bristles. When the dugong presses the disk against the mucky sea floor, it rakes up roots and passes them on to its mouth.

A much smaller animal, the star-nosed mole, slips into streams to grab dinner from the mud. It can't smell or see well, but 22 pink feelers around its nose seem to help it find food such as worms.

The little shrew mole can't see well, so it feels its way by tapping its long nose from side to side.

Insects called weevils have "jaws" on their long noses. Some use them to chew holes in nuts and lay their eggs inside.

A hungry dugong puts its nose to work, pulling out food from the sea floor.

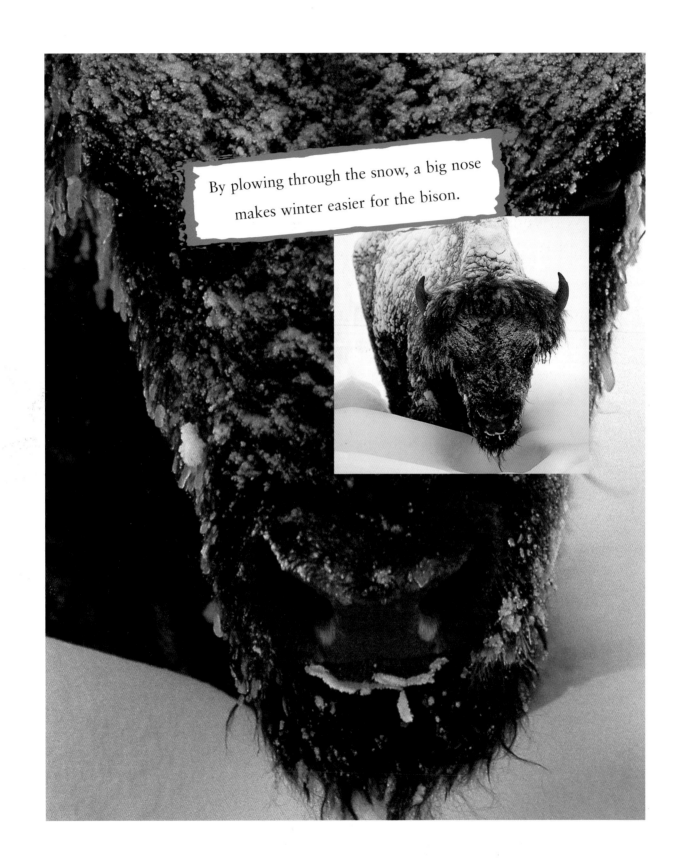

By plowing through the snow, a big nose makes winter easier for the bison.

PLOWING NOSES

If you've ever rubbed your nose against the sand (ouch!), you'll know it's not built for plowing. The tip of your nose bends easily, and the skin that covers it is smooth and soft.

Compare that to the nose of an Australian sand digger called a marsupial (mar-SOO-pee-al) mole. Its nose is furry and has a tough shield of horn for protection. That makes it easy to plow through sand, burrowing for insects and worms. Still, the work must be tiring. After minutes of furious plowing, the mole suddenly falls asleep. Moments later, it lifts its nose and plows again—until the next nap.

The giant bison of North America also plows with its nose, but usually through snow. It throws its heavy weight behind its nose to

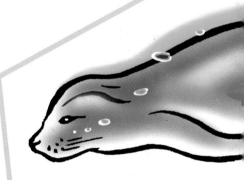

Seals have streamlined snouts, great for diving into deep seas.

plow through deep snow along its winter trails. Sometimes, its strong neck muscles swing its nose from side to side so the bison can dig down to the grass below. It can plow through more than a meter (about 3 feet) of snow to reach food.

The big "nose" of a whale is well designed for plowing through the ocean. Water flows easily over the smooth bullet shape of the whale's entire front end. That helps this heavy animal swim for long distances without using a lot of energy. And its nostrils, called blowholes, are set out of the way—right on top of its head. It's handy to have them there when the whale comes to the surface to breathe.

Killer whales can nose their way through water for long distances at speeds of 13 kilometers (8 miles) per hour.

The earthworm plows through soil, pushing its nose end into narrow cracks.

Like the bow of a ship, the pointed front end of this minke (MIN-ka) whale helps it slip through the sea.

A really big nose can make a really big noise if it belongs to an elephant seal.

TALKING NOSES

You can talk just by wrinkling up your nose. That's how you say something's yucky. But a wolf might wrinkle up its nose—and bare its teeth—to say something else: "Get out of here. Now."

Noses can do a lot of talking—especially for male animals. In Asia, a male proboscis (pro-BAHS-iss) monkey honks a droopy nose that grows longer as he gets older. Sometimes it grows long enough to dangle below his chin. Whenever the monkey honks his nose, it swells up like a balloon. Scientists aren't sure just what the honking is saying, but it seems to be a good way to call through thick forests.

A male elephant seal uses his thick, trunk-like nose to trumpet. The nose is so long its tip can hang 30 centimeters (12 inches) below his

Leaf-nosed bats make noises with their noses. The echoes help the bats find their way in the dark.

mouth. When it's time to breed, the seal opens his mouth wide, dangles his nose inside, and bellows. The noise bounces around inside his mouth, which makes the sound even louder. That's a great way to scare away other male elephant seals. They can hear the noise more than a kilometer (nearly a mile) away.

When a male mandrill talks with his nose, you can't hear it, but you sure can see it. The nose on this big African baboon—and the swellings on both sides of it—are brightly colored. When the colors deepen, the mandrill is saying he's mad or excited. Oddly enough, he also has a colorful rump, which "talks" the same way as his nose.

Elephants sometimes use their trunks to slap playful elephant calves. "Settle down," they're saying.

Woolly alpaca mothers hum through their noses to talk to their young—starting even before the young are born.

Look a mandrill in the nose if you want to know whether or not he's getting mad.

When a killer whale opens its blowhole
to blast out warm, moist air, it looks
as if it's spouting water.

CLOSING NOSES

You might pinch your nose when you jump into a lake. That helps keep the water out. But some animals have a better system: their nostrils can close up by themselves.

As an Australian platypus (PLAT-i-pus) hunts through the water for shrimp, flaps of skin seal its nose shut—and its ears and eyes, too. Then the platypus can't smell, hear, or see much. But it can sense the electric charges that shrimp make with their tails and follow them.

Some kinds of whales have one blowhole on their heads; others have two. But all kinds close these special nostrils to keep out water when they're under the sea. After they rise to the surface, the whales let stale air out and take fresh air in. Then nerves in their skin

The nostrils of a sea-going dugong sit on top of its snout for easier breathing. Underwater, flaps shut them tightly.

trigger muscles that close the blowholes as they dive again.

Water isn't the only thing that might get into a nose. In North America, sand lizards dive into loose sand to escape their enemies and high heat. Their nostrils and ears close to keep them from filling with sand.

The nose on a camel shuts out blowing sand and—in some places—blowing snow. Camel nostrils are long, narrow slits. Special little muscles close them up tight for as long as necessary. Then the camel breathes through its mouth, which is protected by big, floppy lips. If any sand or snow manages to slip through the nostrils, the camel has nose hairs—just like you do—to help filter it out.

Nostrils that close are useful for seals that dive deep and stay underwater for an hour.

Beavers spend a lot of time in water, so it's a good thing their nostrils can close.

18

Having slits for nostrils works well for a camel. It can easily close them to keep out sand or snow.

In rainy seasons, the tenrec in Africa comes out of its tunnel and noses around for food.

POKING NOSES

You might poke your nose into someone else's business. But you wouldn't want to poke it where some animals do. Many kinds of pigs stick their tough, round noses right into the dirt. That's how they find food. Using their great sense of smell, the pigs find the best spots to dig. Then they shovel with their noses to dig out roots, insects, snails, eggs, snakes, and almost anything else they discover. But in spite of what people say about "eating like pigs," wild pigs don't often overeat.

The Mexican long-nosed bat pries open blossoms with a flap on the top of its nose. Then it feeds on nectar and pollen.

Little shrews called tenrecs can't see very well, but their long, pointed noses make great sniffers. They spend most of their time poking their noses into layers of dead leaves to find food. Some kinds of tenrecs prefer to poke into soft mud along streams. Insects and other tiny animals make up most of their meals.

You can guess where a giant anteater sticks its l-o-n-g nose. It sniffs out a nest of ants or termites, tears a hole in the nest, and shoves its nose right in. Holding the nose in place, the anteater flicks its worm-shaped tongue in and out. With each lick, it captures hundreds of insects. But it can barely eat for half a minute at a time. It must stop to scratch all the insect bites it gets. As soon as the anteater empties one nest, it moves onto the next, pokes its nose in, and starts over again. After all, it takes thousands of ants to fill one giant anteater in a night.

The white rhinoceros sometimes uses its front nose horn to dig out roots for dinner.

A walrus sticks its nose into the mud on the sea floor to find shellfish to eat.

This giant anteater of Brazil follows
its nose from ant nest to ant nest.

Watch out! This black rhinoceros in Africa can do a lot of damage—even to a truck.

DEFENDING NOSES

Your nose might save your life by warning you of fire. But don't count on it to scare away your enemies. For that, you'd need a nose like the one on a special African lizard called a Jackson's chameleon (ka-MEEL-yon). It has three spearlike horns that all point forward. They're great for frightening other animals.

Check out a big rhinoceros to find another scary nose. Depending on the kind of rhinoceros it is, it may have one or two big horns on its nose. The horns are made of the same type of material that your fingernails are made of. They're pointed and sharp. If something—or someone—startles a rhinoceros, it might lower its nose, snort loudly, and charge. But the little eyes on the sides of its head don't see well, and they can't see what's straight ahead. That's why

To escape drying winds, one kind of tree frog crawls into a hole and plugs the opening with its spatula-shaped nose.

25

the rhino often misses hitting its target.

Big, wartlike bumps and sharp, curved tusks make a frightening nose on a warthog. Just the sight of this wild pig is enough to scare away some animals. But it will attack if it must. A mother warthog might try to save her little piglets by chasing away a wild cat, such as a leopard. She might even charge a big elephant that's bothering her young ones. And when she goes to bed, she tucks the piglets safely into a burrow, then backs in herself. That way, the mother warthog can guard the entrance with her awful—but wonderful—nose.

The nose of a white-tailed deer can sense danger long before its eyes or ears can.

Sawfish have snouts like saws with razor-sharp teeth—great for attacking their enemies.

You wouldn't want to rub noses with an African warthog, but you have to admire its gear.

 INDEX

28

Greystone Books
A division of Douglas & McIntyre Ltd.
2323 Quebec Street, Suite 201
Vancouver, British Columbia
V5T 4S7

Canadian Cataloguing in Publication Data

Swanson, Diane, 1944—
   Noses that plow and poke

(Up close)
Includes index.
ISBN 1-55054-715-1 (bound) —-ISBN 1-55054-733-X (pbk.)

   1.   Nose—Juvenile literature. 2. Smell—Juvenile literature. I.
Cowles, Rose, 1967 - II. Title. III. Series: Up close (Vancouver,
B.C.)
QL947.S92 1999   j591.5   C99-910429-2

Library of Congress Cataloguing information is available.

Packaged by House of Words for Greystone Books
Editing by Carolyn Bateman
Cover photograph by Frans Lanting / Minden Pictures–First Light
Cover and interior design by Rose Cowles
Interior illustrations by Rose Cowles

Photo credits:
p. ii Alice Thompson; p. 3 Robert Lankinen; p. 4 Thomas Kitchin; p. 7 Kelvin Aitken;
p. 8 Thomas Kitchin; p. 11 Kelvin Aitken; p. 12 First Light; p. 15 Frank Rossotto;
p. 16 Ron Watts; p. 19 Patrick Morrow; p. 20 Frans Lanting/Minden Pictures; p. 23 Frans
Lanting/Minden Pictures; p. 24 Tom Brakefield; p. 27 Frans Lanting/Minden Pictures

All photographs supplied by First Light with the exception of p. ii

Child models Anthony Fiddler and Kimberley Chung through Coast Extras and Talent

Printed and bound in Hong Kong by C & C Offset Printing Co., Ltd.

The publisher gratefully acknowledges the support of the Canada Council for the Arts and
of the British Columbia Ministry of Tourism, Small Business and Culture. The publisher
also acknowledges the financial support of the Government of Canada through the Book
Publishing Industry Development Program.

Canada